W9-ATD-994

樋口大輔

What is a talent?
Is it a special power?
Is it something only the chosen ones can have?
But, what does it mean to be a chosen one to begin with?
What is the difference between ordinary and extraordinary?

A talent is something one has, which others don't have. Finding that unique something, and nurturing it to blossom. I think that's what talent is.

– Daisuke Higuchi

Daisuke Higuchi's manga career began in 1992 when the artist was honored with third prize in the 43rd Osamu Tezuka Award. In that same year, Higuchi debuted as creator of a romantic action story titled ***Itaru***. In 1998, ***Weekly Shonen Jump*** began serializing ***Whistle!*** Higuchi's realistic soccer manga became an instant hit with readers and eventually inspired an anime series, debuting on Japanese TV in May of 2002.

WHISTLE!
VOL. 12: IN THE DISTANCE

The SHONEN JUMP Manga Edition

STORY AND ART BY
DAISUKE HIGUCHI

English Adaptation/Drew Williams
Translation/Naomi Kokubo
Touch-up Art & Lettering/Jim Keefe
Cover, Graphics & Layout/Sean Lee
Editor/Ian Robertson

Managing Editor/Frances E. Wall
Editorial Director/Elizabeth Kawasaki
VP & Editor in Chief/Yumi Hoashi
Sr. Director of Acquisitions/Rika Inouye
Sr. VP of Marketing/Liza Coppola
Exec. VP of Sales & Marketing/John Easum
Publisher/Hyoe Narita

WHISTLE! © 1998 by Daisuke Higuchi. All rights reserved.
First published in Japan in 1998 by SHUEISHA Inc., Tokyo.
English translation rights in the United States of America and Canada arranged by SHUEISHA Inc. Some scenes have been modified from the original Japanese edition. The stories, characters and incidents mentioned in this publication are entirely fictional.

No portion of this book may be reproduced or transmitted in any form or by any means without written permission from the copyright holders.

Printed in the U.S.A.

Published by VIZ Media, LLC
P.O. Box 77010
San Francisco, CA 94107

SHONEN JUMP Manga Edition
10 9 8 7 6 5 4 3 2 1
First printing, July 2006

www.viz.com

PARENTAL ADVISORY
WHISTLE! is rated A and is suitable for readers of all ages.

www.shonenjump.com

WHISTLE!™
Vol. 12
IN THE DISTANCE
Story and Art by
Daisuke Higuchi

SHŌ
KAZAMATSURI
JOSUI JUNIOR HIGH
SOCCER TEAM
FORWARD
AKIRA
SAIONJI
TSUBASA
SHIINA
TATSUYA
MIZUNO
JOSUI JUNIOR HIGH
SOCCER TEAM
MIDFIELDER

TEPPEI KOIWA

EDOGAWA FIRST JUNIOR HIGH

TAKI SUGIHARA

TAKANAWA JUNIOR HIGH

DAICHI FUWA

JOSUI JUNIOR HIGH SOCCER TEAM

GOAL KEEPER

STORY

TO REALIZE HIS DREAM, SHŌ KAZAMATSURI, A BENCH WARMER AT SOCCER POWERHOUSE MUSASHINOMORI, TRANSFERRED TO JOSUI JUNIOR HIGH SO HE COULD PLAY THE GAME HE LOVES.

JOSUI'S SOCCER TEAM WAS A JOKE UNTIL SOUJŪ MATSUSHITA, A FORMER JAPAN LEAGUE PLAYER, TOOK ON THE COACHING DUTIES. UNDER MATSUSHITA'S GUIDANCE, THE TEAM HAS BECOME A FORCE TO BE RECKONED WITH. THEY BLASTED THROUGH THE DISTRICT PRIMARY TOURNAMENT, DEFEATING RAKUYŌ JUNIOR HIGH BEFORE HOLDING OFF HIBA JUNIOR HIGH TO WIN THE TOURNAMENT FINALS.

JOSUI'S SOCCER TEAM HAS HIT AN ALL-TIME HIGH. WHAT'S NEXT FOR THE TOURNAMENT CHAMPS?

WHISTLE!™

Vol. 12
IN THE DISTANCE

STAGE.99
The Conference over Oden
7

STAGE.100
Family Meeting
29

STAGE.101
Spike
49

STAGE.102
The Day the Select Team Convenes
(IN THE DISTANCE)
71

STAGE.103
Skill Test (First Episode)
91

STAGE.104
Skill Test (Second Episode)
111

STAGE.105
Skill Test (Last Episode)
133

STAGE.106
Lunch Time
153

STAGE.107
Lawn Is a Strong Enemy
171

STAGE.99
The Conference Over Oden
CHIRP CHIRP

YAAAWN
FLOOSH

SLIDE

SHOOP
HM?

HE'S GETTING AN EARLY START AGAIN TODAY.

IT'S BEEN THREE MONTHS SINCE HE MOVED IN WITH ME.

I THOUGHT IT WAS OKAY TO KEEP THIS SECRET FROM HIM.
BUT...

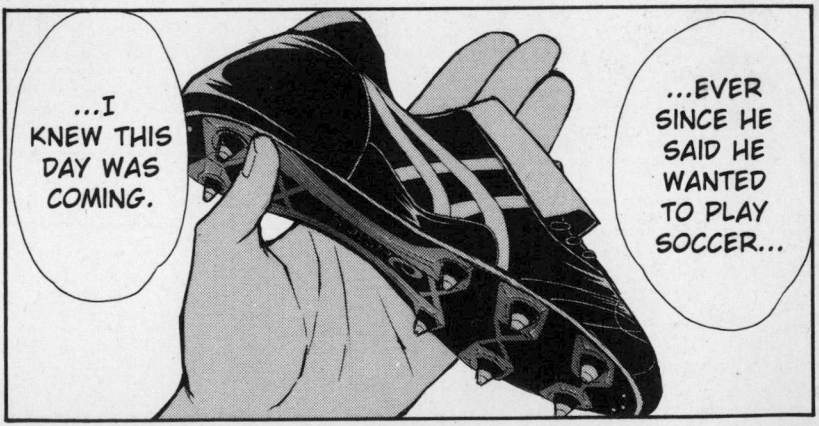
...I KNEW THIS DAY WAS COMING.
...EVER SINCE HE SAID HE WANTED TO PLAY SOCCER...

STAGE.99 The Conference Over Oden

AT FIRST...
FWUMP
...DID I BEGIN TO THINK THAT ISN'T ENOUGH?
...SINCE WHEN...
...I JUST WANTED TO GET IN THERE AND KICK THE BALL, BUT...
SHEESH!
FLUSH
I'M GOING TO WIN THIS GAME!

SHŌ KAZAMATSURI, THAT...WAS LAME.
AFTER ALL, WITHOUT TATSUYA'S HELP, I WOULDN'T HAVE SCORED AT ALL, AND THAT SECOND GOAL WAS JUST DUMB LUCK.
PRETTY ARROGANT.
SKITTER
I CAN'T LET PEOPLE GET INTO MY HEAD WITH...
...FOULS OR MALICIOUS PLAYS.
I GOTTA GET BETTER!

I'M HOME.
AND I AM RIPE.

TH
OOK
TOUGHEN UP!

HISS
POP
WELCOME HOME.

KLINK

COULDN'T SLEEP. BREAKFAST IS READY. WHY DON'T YOU HIT THE SHOWER?
WHAT'S UP BRO?
OKAY.

THANKS FOR THE GRUB.
SHŌ...
...STARTED PLAYING SOCCER, AN AUNT TOLD ME THAT I COULDN'T FIGHT MY NATURE.
WHEN I...
HOW LONG... HAVE YOU KNOWN?
Shō
Kō
Pa
2nd Son Adopted
1st Son
Wife
Self
THEN, WHEN I TRANSFERRED SCHOOLS, I SAW OUR FAMILY REGISTRY, AND THE PIECES CAME TOGETHER.
AT FIRST, I DIDN'T KNOW WHAT SHE WAS TALKING ABOUT, BUT...
...WE WERE TOLD ALL THE TIME THAT WE'RE NOT ALIKE, EVEN THOUGH WE'RE BROTHERS.
BUT IT DOESN'T MEAN SQUAT!
SHŌ, LISTEN...

MY FATHER IS MAMORU KAZAMATSURI. MY MOTHER IS REIKO KAZAMATSURI.
MY BROTHER IS KŌ KAZA-MATSURI.
THAT'S THE WAY I WANT IT.

GOTTA GO.
OOPS, LEMME CLEAN UP.
IT'S OKAY. I'LL TAKE CARE OF THAT.
SCOOT
TAP TAP

AH...
IT'S GETTING LATE!
SCOOT

HE'S TRYING TO SPARE OUR FEELINGS.
CREEK

I'M SURE HE WANTS TO KNOW ABOUT HIS REAL PARENTS.

THAT IS SO WRONG!
SEE YA, LOSER. I'M OFF TO HAWAII.
OH YEAH! IT'S SUMMER VACATION!

TRYING TO SKIP OUT, SHIGEKI?
JOLT

SNEAK

SHIGEKI, LET'S HEAD TO THE MEETING ...
HUH? HE'S GONE?

WE WON'T LET YOU GET AWAY, 'CAUSE YOU'RE THE STAR OF THE SHOW TODAY.
C'MON, IT HURTS!
T... TATSU-BOY.
SQUEEZE

MA-SATO...

HOWZAT, GIMPY?
ENOUGH!

SHUN

LET'S START THE MEETING. IT'S ALSO AN OPPORTUNITY TO REFLECT UPON YESTERDAY'S GAME.
HEY!

I WAS THINKING SELFISHLY...
...WITHOUT CONSIDERING HOW THE OTHERS WOULD TAKE IT.

!
HE HEARD FROM SANTA THAT YOU DELIBERATELY MISSED THE PENALTY.
I SHOULDN'T FEEL DEPRESSED.

WHY ARE WE BEING SINGLED OUT?
WELL, HERE'S A QUESTION FOR YOU: WHO BROUGHT PERSONAL BAGGAGE INTO AN IMPORTANT MATCH...WITH THE CHAMPIONSHIP AT STAKE?
FIDGET
FIDGET
NOT AT ALL.
DON'T YOU GET IT?

HE STAYED UP ALL NIGHT THINKING ABOUT IT, BUT HE COULDN'T FIND AN ANSWER.

YOU MORON!
... FORGET THAT YOU HAVE A WHOLE TEAM BEHIND YOU!
DON'T YOU DARE...
MASATO ...
IT'S SO LIKE YOU... I CAN'T EVEN GET ANGRY ANYMORE.
SHEESH.
START RUNNING!
YUK!
HUH?
DID YOU THINK I'D FORGIVE YOU JUST LIKE THAT?

YOU TWO...HOOF IT AROUND THE SCHOOL GROUNDS 50 TIMES!! THAT WILL SETTLE THE MATTER.
OKAY!
BUT I'M AN INJURED MAN.
PICK UP THE PACE, GIRLS!

YOU'VE GOT 25 LAPS TO GO!
IT'S NO GOOD. I'D LIKE A REDUCED SENTENCE OF 30 LAPS PLEASE.
FUMP
GEEZ, HE RUNS AS IF HE'S ACTUALLY ENJOYING IT.

AND YOU'RE ONE OF THEM. RIGHT, SHIGEKI?

JOSUI IS A DECENT TEAM.

YOU'RE PRETTY GOOD AT DODGING PEOPLE.
WHY DON'T YOU TRY FACING THEM HEAD ON?

IT'S NO JOKE..
PUNK!
GOSH, COACH, HOW 'BOUT A HUG?

IS BIG BRO HOME?
YUKI! WATCH YOUR MANNERS!
SCAMPER
GOOD, YOU'RE HERE...
I'M HOME.
CLIK
BRO!
YOU'RE HOME.
YO.

YOU MEAN IT!?
IT'S BEEN A WHILE...YOU WANNA PLAY SOME BALL?

GOOD TO SEE YOU. ♡ HOW LONG ARE YOU HERE?
HEY, EASY ON THE NECK.
TWO OR THREE DAYS. THE DAY AFTER TOMORROW IS THE VERDY MATCH.
I'LL BE THERE!

YOU KNOW A PLAYER NAMED KENSUKE SHIOMI?
SHIOMI?

WHOOSH
LET ME GET CHANGED!
MAKE SURE YOU TELL MOM.

BY THE WAY, ANIKI...
HMM?

NEVER HEARD OF HIM. WHICH TEAM DOES HE PLAY FOR?
DON'T KNOW. I GUESS HE PLAYED, LIKE, 14 OR 15 YEARS AGO.
IF THAT'S THE CASE, I DON'T HAVE A CLUE.

WELL, IT'S JUST THAT...
HE'S MY FATHER.

COACHES AND SOME OF THE VETS MAY KNOW HIM, BUT...
...WHAT ABOUT HIM?

ODEN

IT REALLY HIT HOME IN THE LAST WORLD CUP...

COMPARED TO THE REST OF THE WORLD, JAPANESE SOCCER HAS SUCH A SHORT HISTORY AND...
...THAT JAPAN LACKS EXPERIENCE.

PRACTICALLY SPEAKING, WHAT DO YOU HAVE IN MIND?

...THERE ARE MANY THINGS TO BE DONE, SUCH AS STRENGTHENING THE J-LEAGUE, BUT...
...THE KEY THING IS TO CREATE A GOOD ENVIRONMENT FOR THE SPORT AND NURTURE YOUNG PLAYERS.

A SELECT TEAM FROM TOKYO.
I WANT TO PUT TOGETHER A TEAM OF TALENTED YOUNG PLAYERS, AND GIVE THEM A CHANCE TO COMPETE ON THE WORLD STAGE.

GRIN
I'VE ALREADY WORKED UP A ROSTER.

WHISTLE!™

STAGE.100

Family
Meeting

I WONDER WHERE HE'S TAKING ME.
HE'S BEEN QUIET FOR A WHILE.

SHIFT

LET'S HANG OUT LATER TODAY, OKAY?

HUH? THIS PLACE!?

YOU LOOK WELL, KŌ.
WHAT'S HAPPENED TO YOUR HAIR?
YOUR FATHER...
...LIKES TO BARK, BUT HE WAS SO HAPPY TO HEAR FROM YOU. HE JUMPED ON THE FIRST PLANE TO COME HERE.
STOMP
STOMP
LOOKS LIKE YOU'RE DOING OKAY FOR YOURSELF.
IF YOU'D TOLD ME, I WOULD HAVE COME TO PICK YOU UP.
IS THAT A PROBLEM?
YOU GUYS ARE EARLY.
NO NEED. WE'RE NOT KIDS.
GRR

HE HASN'T COME HOME FROM PRACTICE, YET.
MAYBE I SHOULDN'T HAVE TOLD THEM...
TEA, PLEASE.
BY THE WAY, WHERE'S SHŌ?
FUMP

LET'S RELAX AND CHAT.
IT'S BEEN A WHILE SINCE WE SAW YOU LAST.

IT'S OKAY.
LET ME HELP YOU.
GUSH

BURBLE BURBLE

TOK
TOK
TOK

CHILL
ARE YOU MAKING ENOUGH TO EAT?
I DO OKAY.
I HEAR THAT THE BAR BUSINESS IS QUITE LUCRATIVE.
WELL, IT'S SO-SO.
I DON'T APPROVE OF YOU MAKING A LOT OF EASY MONEY WHILE YOU'RE STILL YOUNG.
CHILL
BUT...

HE'S GOT A GOOD HEART, AND...

...BECAUSE I DROPPED OUT OF SCHOOL...
...SHŌ HAD TO CARRY THE BURDEN OF YOUR EXPECTATIONS.
I FEEL BAD ABOUT THAT.

...HIS DESIRE TO PLEASE HIS PARENTS AND HIS WISH TO PLAY SOCCER.
...THAT'S WHY HE HAD TO STRUGGLE BETWEEN ...

IT SEEMED LIKE SHŌ DIDN'T KNOW WHAT TO DO WITH HIMSELF. HE HAD A PASSION FOR SOCCER INSIDE HIM, AND HE DIDN'T KNOW WHERE IT CAME FROM.

HE MIGHT HAVE FELT...
... OBLIGATED BECAUSE HE KNEW HE WAS ADOPTED.

SHIOMI ...
...USED TO LAUGH ABOUT HOW SOCCER WAS THE ONLY THING HE KNEW...
...AND WHENEVER HE PLAYED WITH HIS SON, IT NATURALLY INVOLVED SOCCER.

GUESS THE APPLE DOESN'T FALL TOO FAR FROM THE TREE.

SHIOMI KENSUKE WAS...
...A GOOD-HEARTED, DECENT, YOUNG MAN.

HE WAS PLAYING SOCCER BEFORE HE COULD WALK...
...IT'S INEVITABLE THAT HE WOULD BE DRAWN TO IT.

WHEN MY YOUNGER SISTER, KAORI, SAID SHE WAS GOING TO MARRY A SOCCER PLAYER, I WAS VIOLENTLY AGAINST IT.
IT WAS BEFORE THE J-LEAGUE WAS ESTABLISHED. IT'S DIFFERENT TODAY. IT JUST WASN'T A PROPER CAREER BACK THEN.
BUT, EVEN THOUGH I FOUGHT THE MARRIAGE... AS I GOT TO KNOW HIM, I GRADUALLY LEARNED TO ACCEPT HIM.
WE HAD JUST BECOME CLOSE... THEN THE ACCIDENT HAPPENED.
THEY WERE ON THEIR WAY TO THE AIRPORT FOR AN AWAY GAME.
SHŌ HAD JUST TURNED TWO. WE TOOK HIM IN AND RAISED HIM AS OUR OWN SON.
TO ME, SOCCER ONLY MEANS SADNESS.
I THOUGHT IT WOULD BE BETTER TO FORGET ABOUT IT AND GET ON WITH OUR LIVES.

BUT, I'D SAY IT'S ABOUT TIME...
...TO RELEASE WHAT'S BEEN BOTTLED UP ALL THIS TIME.

SWISH

WHAT DO YOU WANT, OLD MAN !?

SN
EER
OH. MY IDIOT SON TAGGED ALONG?

COME ON IN, SHŌ.
WEREN'T YOU THE ONE WHO ASKED ME TO BRING SHŌ OVER, MEIN FUHRER?

WHAT ON EARTH ...
...IS GOING ON NOW?

HAVE YOU HAD DINNER YET?
NOT YET.

SUPER-8?
THERE'S SOMETHING I WANT TO SHOW SHŌ.
THIS IS RARE FOOTAGE.
IT'S SOMETHING THAT'S BEEN PRESERVED AS A COACHING TOOL.
2

I WAS 12 THEN.
MY FATHER TOOK ME TO WATCH...
...THE JAPAN LEAGUE MATCH BETWEEN SHINKAWA DENKŌ VS. YAMATO MOTOR.

YAMATO MOTOR WAS DEFEATED 2 TO 1.
BUT WHAT I REMEMBER WAS A NEARLY ZERO-DEGREE SHOT ON GOAL.
THE IMAGE OF THE PLAYER WHO PULLED OFF THAT GOAL...

AT THAT MOMENT, MY OBSESSION WITH SOCCER BEGAN.
...WAS BURNED INTO MY MEMORY AND NEVER FADES.
EVEN NOW, WHEN I THINK ABOUT IT, I GET THE SAME BURNING SENSATION DOWN MY SPINE.

...AND RELENTLESS *TENACITY* IN GETTING TO THE BALL.
KENSUKE SHIOMI POSSESSED A STRIKER'S MOST IMPORTANT GIFTS: A RADAR-LIKE "SENSE OF WHERE YOU ARE" ON THE PITCH.

...UNTIL HE DIED YOUNG IN AN AUTOMOBILE ACCIDENT.
HE WAS ONE OF THE MOST PROMISING STRIKERS OF HIS GENERATION ...

READ THIS WAY
WILL YOU... WILL YOU LET ME WATCH ONE MORE TIME?
E...EXCUSE ME, COACH!
YOU CAN WATCH AS MANY TIMES AS YOU LIKE.
CLICK
LET'S GIVE HIM A MINUTE.
GET OFF ME!
I'LL BET YOU'VE NEVER SEEN HIM PLAY BEFORE, RIGHT?
... THAT'S TRUE.

THANK YOU SO MUCH FOR TODAY, TATSUYA.

SOME-HOW, I'M STILL ...
...NOT SURE. BUT IT'S A GREAT CHANCE... FOR ME.

YOU'RE GOING TO GO, RIGHT?

I'M SURE YOU'LL BE OFFICIALLY NOTIFIED, BUT...

SEE YOU TOMORROW, THEN.

FROM JOSUI, WE PICKED...
...WE'RE PUTTING TOGETHER A SELECT TEAM.

...AND DAICHI FUWA AS GOAL KEEPER.
... TATSUYA AND YOU, SHŌ...

WHAT?

CLICK
YOU'RE HOME.
I'M... SELECTED!?
!
DAD?!
MOM, TOO?!

WHISTLE!

STAGE.101 Spike

STAGE.101
Spike

YOU HAVE A TAN, SHŌ.

...YOU LOOK A LOT OLDER. THE LAST TIME WE SAW YOU WAS WHEN YOU ENTERED MUSASHINOMORI, I THINK.
MAYBE THAT'S THE REASON...

DAD.
IN FACT, I WAS...

I'M RELIEVED TO SEE YOU SO HEALTHY.
DAD...

...

READ THIS WAY
WHAT?
WE RECEIVED THE NOTICE A LITTLE WHILE AGO.
IT SOUNDS LIKE YOU'LL BE PLAYING MORE SOCCER THAN EVER.
YOU WERE CHOSEN FOR SOME SORT OF SELECT TEAM, RIGHT?
I KNOW ABOUT IT.
...YOU'VE COME A LONG WAY, I'D SAY.
WITHOUT OUR INVOLVEMENT ...
I'D GRADUATE FROM A GOOD SCHOOL, GET A PROPER JOB, AND LIVE A NORMAL LIFE...
...COULD, I WOULD FULFILL YOUR WISHES.
... BUT...
I'M SORRY.
DAD, IF I...

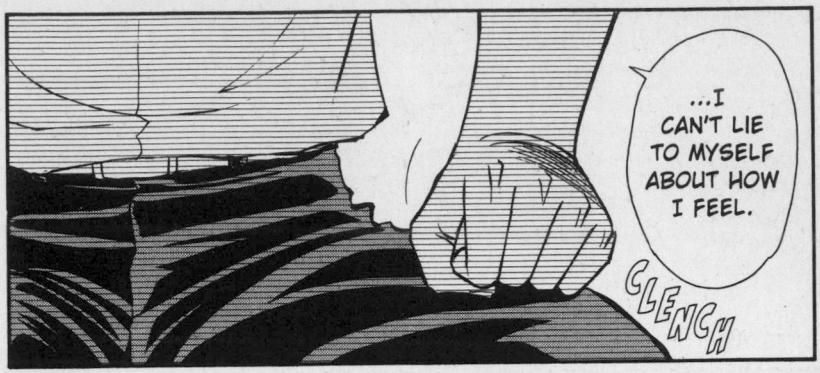

I WANT TO PLAY SOCCER.

I LOVE SOCCER.

AS LONG AS I BREATHE...

...I WANT TO PLAY.

THERE ARE MILLIONS OF KIDS WHO FEEL THAT WAY.
BUT NOT EVERYONE CAN MAKE A LIVING AS A SOCCER PLAYER.
DO YOU THINK YOU HAVE THE TALENT?
I DON'T KNOW.
BUT, UNLESS I TRY...
EVEN IF YOU MAKE IT AND BECOME A PRO...
...IT'S A TOUGH LIFE. NOT EVERYONE CAN BECOME A STAR PLAYER.
BEHIND THE BRIGHT LIGHTS AND MAGAZINE COVERS, THERE ARE MANY PLAYERS WHO JUST VANISH INTO OBSCURITY.
NO ONE CAN HELP YOU! YOU'LL HAVE TO DO IT ALL ON YOUR OWN! JUST WANTING IT WON'T MAKE IT HAPPEN. IT'S A CRUEL WORLD.
...
I KNOW.

THIS ISN'T ABOUT THE FACT THAT MY FATHER WAS A SOCCER PLAYER.

EVEN THOUGH ***MY FATHER WAS A SOCCER PLAYER...***

I WANT TO DO THIS BECAUSE I LOVE PLAYING SOCCER.
YES.
I'M SORRY.
PEOPLE DIE IF THEY CANNOT BREATHE.
SOCCER IS LIKE THAT FOR ME.
WHAT !?
HOW DARE YOU SAY THAT.
I CAN'T PROMISE THAT, BUT I WON'T THROW AWAY SOCCER JUST FOR KAORI'S SAKE EITHER.
SLAM
WITH THAT KIND OF JOB, CAN YOU MAKE MY SISTER HAPPY?
IT'S AN UNSTABLE CAREER, AND THERE ARE NO GUARANTEES.

WHEN HE LOOKS SO HAPPY, HOW CAN I STOP HIM?
KENSUKE, HE IS YOUR SON AFTER ALL.
BROTHER.
THEY'RE USABLE.
THAT'S WHAT KŌ SAID.
BUT THEY AREN'T USABLE, ARE THEY?
THEY'RE MY BEST CLEATS FOR RAIN.
I MEAN, THE PAIR OF SHOES I BOUGHT FOR YOU WHEN YOU WERE ACCEPTED BY MUSASHI-NOMORI.
YOU STILL KEPT THOSE!?
I DIDN'T EXPECT THAT SOMEONE ...
...WHO DISLIKES SOCCER SO MUCH WOULD BUY ME SOMETHING LIKE THAT.
SO, THEY'RE IMPORTANT TO ME.
ASICS

...SHŌ.
THAT REMINDS ME...
YOU STILL THINK OF ME AS YOUR FATHER, THEN.
...WE BROUGHT SOMETHING FOR YOU.
KENSUKE SHIOMI, YOUR BIOLOGICAL FATHER, USED TO WEAR THESE.
WHAT'S THAT?

IF YOU'RE WILLING TO TRY THIS PATH, GIVE IT YOUR BEST SHOT.
I WON'T TRY TO CONTROL YOU ANYMORE. IT'S YOUR LIFE.
UM, AND YOU HAD BETTER NOT QUIT UNTIL YOU SUCCEED!
BUT, IN EXCHANGE, I WON'T TOLERATE ANY WHINING FROM YOU!

WE ALSO WANT TO PROTECT THEM FROM HARDSHIP... IF WE CAN HELP IT.
ALL PARENTS WANT THEIR CHILDREN TO BE HAPPY.
BUT ...

WELL... WHY DON'T WE HAVE SOME DINNER?
HEY, STOP HUGGING ME!
THANK YOU, DAD!

MOM.

MOM...
THE DINNER HAS GONE COLD. I'D BETTER WARM IT UP.
...THAT'S ENOUGH.
... BASICALLY, AS LONG AS OUR CHILDREN ARE HEALTHY...
DASH
AH, JUST A SEC.
THEN, WILL YOU PUT THE DISHES OUT?
LET ME HELP YOU.
I HAVE TWO FATHERS AND TWO MOTHERS.
FUMP
I GUESS THEY GOT A LOT OF USE.
WHEW! THEY STINK.

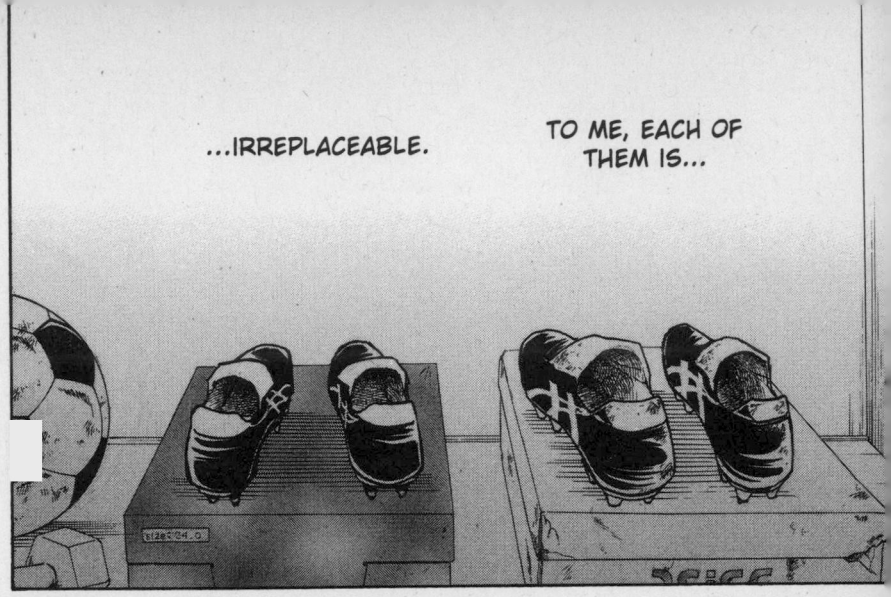
...IRREPLACEABLE.
TO ME, EACH OF THEM IS...

SELECT TEAM, HUH?
...SHŌ, WHO REALLY STANK UNTIL RECENTLY, WAS ALSO PICKED. THAT'S A BIG SURPRISE...
TATSUYA'S CASE IS UNDER-STANDABLE, BUT...
...I MEAN, A SHOCK, DON'T YOU THINK?

YOU KNOW, WHY SHOULD I KEEP KILLING MYSELF IN PRACTICE?
...THEY'RE GOING TO BE PRACTICING WITH THE SELECT TEAM AT THE SAME TIME WE'RE TRAINING FOR THE CHAMPIONSHIP, RIGHT?
DIDN'T THEY SAY THEY'RE STARTING A THREE-DAY RETREAT TOMORROW? EVEN THOUGH WE'VE GOT A LITTLE TIME BEFORE THE CHAMPIONSHIP...
...IF WE LOSE ONCE DURING THE CHAMPIONSHIP, THAT'S THE END OF IT FOR US...
I KNOW THAT, BUT...
THAT'S RIGHT.
BUT IT'S NOT LIKE SHŌ IS GOING TO LEAVE JOSUI.
...DON'T YOU THINK ALL THIS SELECT TEAM STUFF SORT OF UNDERMINES OUR OWN TEAM SPIRIT?
...WHILE SHŌ AND THE OTHERS STILL HAVE THE SELECT TEAM TO FALL BACK ON.
WE'VE BEEN WORKING TOGETHER TO DEFEAT MUSASHINOMORI UP UNTIL NOW, BUT...

I'D SAY THAT'S A VERY JAPANESE WAY OF THINKING.
YOU DON'T LIKE IT UNLESS WE SHARE EVERYTHING THE SAME, HUH?
CRUNCH
SHIGEKI!?
...WOULD BE TOO RISKY TO HAVE ON THE TEAM. IF I WERE IN CHARGE, I'D DO THE SAME THING.
SOMEONE LIKE ME...SOMEONE UNPREDICTABLE...
IT'S JUST LIKE GAMBLING.
NOT SURPRISING.
AREN'T YOU UPSET? AFTER ALL, SHŌ WAS CHOSEN AND YOU WEREN'T!
BUT WHAT ABOUT YOU?

IF YOU DON'T BRING YOUR "A" GAME TO THAT TEAM, YOU'LL BE CRUSHED BY MORE POWERFUL PLAYERS. IT'S POTENTIALLY DEVASTATING.
BEING CHOSEN FOR THE SELECT TEAM DOESN'T MEAN THEY'LL BE TREATED WELL.

MAMORU, YOU'RE MISTAKEN ABOUT ONE THING.

WITH NUISANCE BOY OUT OF THE WAY, NOTHING CAN STOP MY ♡ FOR MIYUKI.

...BUT THEY'LL ALSO BE ROUGHING IT WITH THE SELECT TEAM. THEIR SCHEDULE WILL BE BRUTAL.
NOT ONLY WILL THEY HAVE TO PRACTICE WITH US ...

HE HELPED ME IMPROVE, TOO.
...TRAINS IN THE MORNING AND AT NIGHT EVERYDAY... ON TOP OF OUR REGULAR PRACTICES.

HE...

I LIKE SOCCER, BUT...
...SHŌ IS OBSESSED WITH IT.
I COULD NEVER DO AS MUCH AS HE DOES.
I WOULD NEVER DREAM OF MAKING A LIVING AS A SOCCER PLAYER.
ONCE I GROW UP, I'LL EVENTUALLY INHERIT DAD'S STORE...AND I'LL, YOU KNOW, PLAY SOCCER...AS A HOBBY.
SHŌ IS ON ANOTHER LEVEL.
IT'S A TOUGH PILL TO SWALLOW BUT...
...I WANT TO SUPPORT HIM BECAUSE... THAT'S JUST WHO HE IS!

YEAH.

HE PULLED US ALONG...
...AND HELPED US TO GET TO WHERE WE ARE.

SHŌ AND THE OTHERS WILL RETURN AFTER THEIR TIME WITH THE SELECT TEAM.

DON'T THINK YOU GUYS CAN RELAX.
WHEN THEY COME BACK, THEY'LL BE STRONGER.
I WILL PUSH YOU JUST AS HARD AS SHŌ AND THE OTHERS WILL BE PUSHED. PREPARE YOUR-SELVES!

FOR THE SELECT TEAM RETREAT EPISODE, I VISITED AND RESEARCHED J VILLAGE IN FUKUSHIMA, WHICH IS A FAMOUS RETREAT FOR THE JAPAN REPRESENTATIVE TEAM.

I APPRECIATED THEIR HOSPITALITY.

J Village

IT'S A NATIONAL TRAINING CENTER FOR SOCCER: A WELL-EQUIPPED FACILITY THAT INCLUDES A STADIUM WITH NATURAL GRASS, A HUGE TRAINING GROUND AND LODGING FACILITIES.

STAGE.102 The Select Team Convenes (IN THE DISTANCE)

STAGE.102

The Select Team Convenes (IN THE DISTANCE)

WHAT'S HE DOING?
IT FEELS GREAT!

SHFF

I FEEL THE SAME WAY.

THE LAWN IS NICE, HUH?

SIGH
LOOK AT THEM!
YUP.
GO BACK TO THE TRAILER PARK!
LOSERS.
THEY'RE GETTING EXCITED ABOUT THE FREAKIN' LAWN.

SNORT

BURN
I BET THEY JUST WANT TO BE OUR BUDDIES. DON'T YOU THINK?
I THINK THEY'RE TALKING ABOUT US.
HEH HEH

HEY, YOU GUYS!

SNEER

IT MUST BE DISCONCERTING TO INVENT SUCH A CLEVER PUTDOWN, THEN SEE IT BACKFIRE.
HEH

LITTLE PUNKS!!
TRESPASSERS ARE NOT ALLOWED IN HERE! GET OUT!
SORRY ABOUT SHOUTING. WELCOME TO YOU, J-LEAGUERS OF THE FUTURE!
SAME HERE.
WE'RE NOT TRESPASSERS. WE CAME HERE FOR THE SELECT TEAM RETREAT.
OH, IS THAT SO?
WHAT!?
YOU?
I'M SORRY.

AH...
205
SHŌ KAZAMATSURI
TEPPEI KOIWA
TAKI SUGIHARA
DAICHI FUWA

IT'S BIG.
AND NICE.

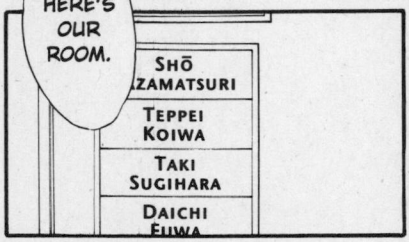
HERE'S OUR ROOM.
SHŌ KAZAMATSURI
TEPPEI KOIWA
TAKI SUGIHARA
DAICHI FUWA

OKAY.
205
SHŌ KAZAMATSURI
TEPPEI KOIWA
TAKI SUGIHARA
DAICHI FUWA
SEE YOU LATER.
I'M IN ANOTHER ROOM.

SWING
GLARE
WHAT'RE YOU LOOKING AT? YOU WANT A BEATDOWN, PRINCESS?
LATCH
205

WHY IS HE SQUATING IN THERE WITH HIS SHIRT OFF?
IT'S NOT THE WRONG ROOM, IS IT?
AH HA HA HA HA

SWING
205
UHHH, SORRY ABOUT THAT.

IT'S KIND OF A SMALL ROOM, BUT COME ON IN.
I MEAN, YOU SEEM FAIRLY NORMAL.
BUT YOU GUYS DON'T LOOK ALL THAT TOUGH.

SO, I TRIED TO PUT MY GAME FACE ON.
I FIGURED SOME HIGH-POWERED GUYS WERE BROUGHT HERE FOR THE SELECT TEAM, RIGHT? GOTTA MAKE THE RIGHT IMPRESSION.

NOW, LET'S INTRODUCE OURSELVES.
SQUEEK
SOUR-PUSS, TAKE THE TOP.
THIS BED IS MINE.
TEENY-WEENY MIDGET BOY, TAKE THE BOTTOM.
KIND OF A CONTROL FREAK ...
DOPEY, YOU, TAKE THIS ONE.

DAICHI FUWA FROM JOSUI JUNIOR HIGH.

I'M TEPPEI KOIWA FROM EDOGAWA FIRST JUNIOR HIGH.
I'M THE ONLY ONE HERE FROM MY SCHOOL.

I'M ALSO FROM JOSUI. SHŌ KAZA-MATSURI.
PLUS THERE'S ANOTHER GUY FROM JOSUI IN ANOTHER ROOM.

I'M FROM TAKANAWA JUNIOR HIGH...
...NAME'S TAKI SUGI-HARA.

COOL, YOU GUYS ARE MY POSSE FOR THREE DAYS.

...MY ROOM-MATES SEEM LIKE NICE GUYS.
I'M A BIT RELIEVED.
I WAS WORRIED ABOUT HOW I WAS GOING GET ALONG WITH THE SELECT PLAYERS, BUT...

...MUST GATHER AT THE MEETING ROOM ON THE FIRST FLOOR.
WE'RE STARTING A MEETING. ALL RETREAT PARTICIPANTS ...

YO, YOU'RE HERE.
SEIJI. KATSURŌ.
AND AKIRA... SHIGERU...
GUESS THEY MADE THE TEAM.
HEY, THAT'S MUSASHI-NOMORI'S KEEPER, KATSURŌ, AND SEIJI, ONE OF THE STRIKERS.
YOU'RE BLOCKING THE WAY. MOVE!
BY THE WAY, WHO IS THAT RUNT TALKING TO THEM?
THERE'S NO WAY THAT GUY IS A SELECT PLAYER...
HEH HEH
WHAT A JOKE!

RYOICHI!?
YO.
HUH?
A GIANT!? WHAT A FREAK.
CAN HE BE A JUNIOR HIGH STUDENT?
WHAT IS IT?
YOU SEEM DIFFERENT.
REALLY?
THIS ISN'T A FAMILY REUNION.
HE'S A LOT MORE CALM.

DON'T GET SO EXCITED.
IT'S WEIRD THAT I WAS SELECTED AND SHIGEKI WASN'T. PROBABLY BECAUSE HIS ARM WAS INJURED...
HE WASN'T SELECTED.
I DON'T SEE THE BLOND ONE.
OH, THE HIBA JUNIOR HIGH PEOPLE.
FHOOSH
OTHER-WISE, YOU PROBABLY WON'T MAKE IT THROUGH THIS RETREAT.
Meeting Room
SOUNDS LIKE YOU RECOGNIZE YOUR PLACE. YOU'D BETTER HOLD ON TO YOUR HUMILTY AND JUST KICK BUTT ON THE FIELD.

WHAT A MOB SCENE.

I MEAN, NOT MAYBE... THEY'RE ALL MEMBERS OF THE SELECT TEAM, RIGHT?
MAYBE ...

YOU'RE LATE! YOU SHOULD BE HERE 10 MINUTES BEFORE THE SCHEDULED TIME.
SORRY.
NEXT TIME, THE ONES WHO CANNOT STRICTLY FOLLOW THE SCHEDULE WILL BE SENT HOME IMMEDIATELY.

I AM THE DRILLS COACH FOR THIS TEAM...
...COACH OBANAZAWA.

ARE THERE ABOUT 40 OF US?
GROUP A IS OVER THERE, AND THE REST ARE WITH B.
SIT OVER HERE.

SAIONJI IS THE HEAD COACH.
THE GOAL KEEPER COACH IS MR. LEWIS.

ULTIMATELY, WE WILL CULL 20 PEOPLE FROM THIS GROUP OF 45 FOR THE TOKYO SELECT TEAM.
THE PURPOSE OF THIS RETREAT IS TO TRAIN YOU AND TEST YOU IN THE FUNDAMENTALS.
YOU'RE WITH GROUP B.
HUH? B?
...AND AS FAR AS I'M CONCERNED, YOU ARE JUST SUB-STITUTES.
ESPECIALLY GROUP B, YOU PLAYERS WERE MERELY RECOMMENDED BY COACH SAIONJI...
TALENT ALONE WILL NOT GUARANTEE YOU A SPOT. KEEP THAT IN MIND, AND WORK HARD.
MORE THAN HALF OF US WILL BE ELIMINATED!
GULP
THAT SAID, DO THE BEST YOU CAN.

WHISTLE!™

STAGE.103
Skill Test (First Episode)

...WE WENT OUT TO THE TRAINING GROUND AND WARMED UP.
THE FIRST DAY OF THE RETREAT. WE ASSEMBLED AT 7:30 IN THE MORNING. THEN AFTER AN 8 A.M. MEETING...

AS SOON AS YOU PUT ON YOUR BIBS, SPLIT UP AND GO TO FIVE DIFFERENT SPOTS TO TAKE THE TESTS.
WE'LL START THE TESTS NOW. THERE ARE FIVE SKILLS TO EVALUATE.

Group A
22
17

ISN'T THIS DISCRIMINATION?
MUTTER MUTTER
Group B
31
20

LET'S GIVE IT OUR BEST SHOT!
DON'T WORRY ABOUT IT. I KNEW WHERE I STOOD...EVEN BEFORE HIS SPEECH.
YOU MEAN, BECAUSE HE SAID WE'RE A BUNCH OF SUBS?
EVEN THOUGH THEY DIVIDED US INTO DIFFERENT GROUPS, DON'T LET IT GET TO YOU.
OOOH! AWESOME!
SEIJI FROM MUSASHINOMORI RAN THE 50 METER DASH IN SIX SECONDS FLAT. HE SMOKED 'EM...THEY WERE NOWHERE NEAR HIM.
THE OTHER MUSASHI-NOMORI GUYS ARE JUST OVER SIX SECONDS.
NO SURPRISE... MUSASHI-NOMORI IS INCREDIBLE.

MUSASHI-NOMORI ISN'T THAT HOT.
HEH HEH HEH
PUMP PUMP
...THE EDOGAWA FLASH DOES IT!
CHECK OUT HOW THE MAN KNOWN AS...
TEPPEI ...
WHAT THE...HE'S RUNNING BARE-FOOT.
HE'S ONLY ON THE B TEAM. WHAT'S HE TALKING ABOUT?
TWEE

DA
SH
SHEESH!
I'M NOT GONNA LET SOME B TEAMER BEAT ME!
VOO
SH

CLICK
ZOOM

OHHH!
INCREDIBLE.
HE DASHES LIKE A COCKROACH.
WOULDN'T HE BE BETTER OFF IN TRACK AND FIELD?
WHOA. SCARY.
FIVE-POINT-NINE-O.

SIX-POINT-FIVE-SIX.

SEVEN-POINT-TWO-THREE.

IT WAS AN EASY WIN. GOOD LUCK, YOU GUYS!
... THANKS.

Server
OVER HERE, WE'LL TEST YOUR BALL CONTROL.
5 meters.
5 m

ONE...
...AND YOU TRAP IT...

THE SERVER THROWS THE BALL ...

EVEN IF YOU RETURN WITH TWO TOUCHES, IF YOU CAN'T RETURN IT ACCURATELY TO THE SERVER...
... YOU'LL LOSE A POINT.

SEE, HE LOST ONE POINT.
AH.
IF YOU STEP OUT OF THE CIRCLE, YOU'LL LOSE A POINT.

TWO ...
...THEN SEND IT BACK TO THE SERVER WITH TWO TOUCHES.
THAT'LL GIVE YOU TWO POINTS.

IF YOU STAY FOCUSED, I'M SURE YOU CAN DO IT.
PSST
AS A MATTER OF FACT, I STINK AT BALL CONTROL.

GUHH
EACH PLAYER GETS FIVE TRIES. ANYONE WITH A SCORE AT OR BELOW FIVE MUST RUN AROUND THE FIELD FIVE TIMES.

BURN
THE GUY I JUST BEAT!
AH!
18

20
20

DON'T GET TOO FULL OF YOURSELF, SUBSTITUTE!
TWEE
20

BURN
THIS IS JUST A BASIC SKILL.
TEN POINTS.
YES.
SWIP
NEXT.
TEN POINTS.

THAT ONE... HE'S REALLY GOOD.
NEXT!
WHOOP ...
FOOSH

LET'S ...
... REDO ...
AH.
I'M SORRY, IT SLIPPED!

TUMP
...THAT TERRIBLE THROW.
INCREDIBLE. HE ACCURATELY TRAPPED AND RETURNED...
NICE PASS.
HMPH
HE'S KAKU EISHI OF ZŌSHIGAYAMINAMI JUNIOR HIGH.
THESE GUYS ARE GOOD! ESPECIALLY THE THIRD ONE.
THE OTHER ONE IS KAZUMA SANADA OF NOGAMIGAOKA JUNIOR HIGH.
THE BROWN-HAIRED ONE IS YŪTO WAKANA OF SETA THIRD JUNIOR HIGH.

THOSE THREE ARE FROM THE CLUB YOUTH, AND...
...THEY'RE FAMOUS IN THE 14-AND-UNDER CIRCUIT.
TAKI, GOOD LUCK.
I WOULDN'T WANT TO TRY IT.
IT'S TOUGH HAVING TO GO RIGHT AFTER THOSE THREE.
YES.
NEXT.
GRIN

BWA HA HA
I'LL BET SOME OF THEM WANT TO GO HOME TO MOMMY AFTER SEEING THE GROUP A HOTSHOTS.
COACH SAIONJI, HOW ARE THE GROUP B GUYS DOING?

WHAT'S GOING ON?
OHH!

HE GOT IT!!
FUMP
THE BALL IS TOO LOW!

SPIN
THOOP
TUMP
AH.
OH.

TUMP
!

WHOOA
INCREDIBLE. HE RETURNED IT FACING THE OPPOSITE WAY.
NICE PASS!

...NOT BAD.
WHAT DO YOU THINK OF THAT BOY?

HMPH.

READ THIS WAY
Y... YES!
WHO'S NEXT?
NEXT!
THEY'RE ALL INCREDIBLE ...
SO LONG AS I STAY FROSTY...I CAN DO IT.
I CAN'T THINK ABOUT THE OTHERS.
BIG SURPRISE... THEY'RE GROUP B.
HOW LAME. SOME OF THEM ACTUALLY HAD TO RUN.
JOG
JOG

GRRR
Ball Control
Shō: 5 points
Teppei: 4 points

...
I'VE GOT MY SPEED.
DANG! WHO CARES ABOUT BALL CONTROL!?

THAT GUY FROM YOUR SCHOOL IS...
... SHOOTING AT THE TARGETS NOW.

I DON'T...

FOOSH
VIP
CHATTER
CHATTER
IF HE GETS ANOTHER ONE, HE'LL HAVE A PERFECT SCORE!
17
29
16
21
30

WHOA
FOOSH
17

WHAT AM I GOING TO DO? COMPARED TO THESE GUYS, THERE'S NOTHING EXCEPTIONAL ABOUT ME.
I'M SCREWED!

STAGE.104

Skill Test (Second Episode)

AKIRA.
HMM.
JUST FINISHING UP THE FOURTH TEST.
MARCO.
GROUP A IS DOING PRETTY WELL ACROSS THE BOARD.
YEP. EACH NEW CROP OF KIDS SEEMS BETTER THAN THE LAST.
HOW'RE THE KIDS DOING?

ON THE OTHER HAND, THE KIDS IN THE GROUP B ARE ALL OVER THE MAP.
IT'S NATURAL. AFTER ALL, EACH OF THOSE PLAYERS ARE EXCEPTIONAL IN JUST ONE AREA.
HE MAY NOT BE GOOD AT BALL CONTROL, BUT HE'S EXTREMELY FAST.
EVEN THOUGH HE HAS TEAMWORK ISSUES, HE'S AN EXCEPTIONAL SHOOTER.
THE KEEPER ISN'T THERE QUITE YET, BUT HE SEEMS TO HAVE INCREDIBLE POTENTIAL.
EVEN THOUGH HE LACKS STAMINA, HE CAN MAKE EXTREMELY ACCURATE PASSES.

NOTHING IN PARTICULAR.
WHAT DID YOU HAVE IN MIND BY MIXING THE GREEN B KIDS WITH THE GROUP A HOT SHOTS, AKIRA?
GOT IT. SO, GROUP B IS MADE UP OF BOYS WITH GOOD POTENTIAL.

AH.
THIS KID, SHŌ KAZAMATSURI, DOESN'T SEEM TO SHINE IN ANY WAY.
HEH HEH

HM?

TECHNIQUE IS SOMETHING HE CAN START LEARNING NOW.

AS FAR AS HE'S CONCERNED, THAT'S FINE.
LEG SPEED, BALL CONTROL, REFLEXES, STRENGTH AND JUMPING POWER.
SO FAR, HE'S SCORING AT THE BOTTOM.

WHAT HE HAS IS SOMETHING ...
...WHICH, SURPRISINGLY, NOT EVEN MANY PROFESSIONAL PLAYERS POSSESS...

...AND IT'S SOMETHING THE ELITE PLAYERS ATTENDING THIS RETREAT LACK.
SOMETHING IMPORTANT.

BUT HE HIMSELF IS NOT AWARE OF IT.
HEY, YOU REALLY STINK!
AH HA HA....
THAT'S AN AMAZING ACCOMPLISHMENT.
CONGRA-TULATIONS. YOU'VE SCORED THE WORST OUT OF EVERYONE.
WHY IS THAT LOSER EVEN HERE?
MR. TSUBASA.
JUST CALL ME TSUBASA.

I BET IT'S A MISTAKE OF SOME SORT.
WHATEVER THE REASON, GROUP B IS A MAJOR ANNOYANCE.
I GUESS THAT CHICK COACH HAS NO EYE, HUH?
...
IF THEY DON'T TAKE COACH SERIOUSLY, THEY'LL BE CRYING LATER.
FULL OF THEM-SELVES.
WE'D BETTER BE CARE-FUL.
AH HA HA HA
PLAYING AGAINST CRAPPY PLAYERS WILL ONLY DRAG US DOWN, TOO.
WHOA.
SWAP

HEY BUDDY...
...ARE YOU FEELING LOW?
N...NO, I...
OF COURSE, YOU SHOULDN'T. I'D UNDERSTAND IF YOU WERE A RESPECTED PLAYER, BUT...
...IT'S A SURPRISE THAT YOU'RE EVEN HERE, RIGHT?
AH.
DEPRESSION IS TOTALLY OUT OF QUESTION.
BLUSH
WHO ARE YOU TO BE DEPRESSED?
YOU'RE RIGHT!

IF I HAD TIME TO FEEL DEPRESSED, THEN I'D BETTER THINK ABOUT MY COMMITMENT TO THE GAME!
YUP.

BUT BECAUSE I WAS SELECTED, I GOT A BIG HEAD.
YEAH?
TO BE HONEST, I ALSO DIDN'T UNDERSTAND WHY I WAS SELECTED.

THANK YOU, MR. TSUBASA.
TSU-BASA.
SOMEHOW, YOU PUT ME OFF BALANCE WHENEVER I TALK TO YOU.
OH WELL. THAT WASN'T EXACTLY THE RESPONSE I WAS SHOOTING FOR, BUT I'LL TAKE WHAT I CAN GET, I GUESS.

I'D SAY THE MEMBERS OF GROUP B ARE COACH AKIRA'S KEY INGREDIENTS.
IT SMELLS LIKE AN EXPERIMENT TO ME.
I BET A LOT OF THESE PEOPLE ARE PUZZLED BY THE SELECTION OF THE TEAM MEMBERS.
23
12

NOTHING.
WHAT'S WRONG, KATSURŌ?

THE GROUP DIVISIONS ARE INTERESTING. "A" CONSISTS OF ELITES WHILE "B" IS FULL OF ODDBALLS. WHAT'RE THESE COACHES TRYING TO COOK UP?
STRANGE THAT TSUBASA OF HIBA JUNIOR HIGH WOULD BE IN GROUP B. AS FAR AS HIS SKILL IS CONCERNED, HE SHOULD BE IN GROUP A.

WE'LL LET YOU TRY SOME THREE-ON-TWO PRACTICE GAMES WITH A DEFENDED GOAL.
THE FIFTH TEST WILL CHECK YOUR COMBINED SKILLS AND YOUR JUDGMENT.

HOWEVER, THERE WILL BE *TWO* KEEPERS.
THERE WILL BE NO TIME LIMIT. THE MOMENT YOU MAKE A GOAL OR A KEEPER CATCHES THE BALL...
...THE GAME WILL END.
NO WAY!
THIS IS AN *IDIOTIC TEST.*
WITH TWO KEEPERS, IT'LL BE IMPOSSIBLE TO SCORE.
YOU'LL GET ONE MINUTE TO DISCUSS YOUR FORMATION.

YOU WON'T KNOW IF IT'S IMPOSSIBLE OR NOT UNTIL YOU TRY.
IF YOU DON'T WANT TO LOSE A POINT, GET STARTED.
I DON'T UNDER-STAND.
WHY ARE THERE TWO KEEPERS?
I SUPPOSE IT'S TO MAKE IT HARDER TO SHOOT, BUT...
...I DON'T UNDERSTAND IT EITHER.
BUT I'M NOT SO SURE ABOUT...
... STANDING SO CLOSE TOGETHER.
LOOM

THOOM
POSE
IS THIS SPOT OKAY, THEN?
NO ...
I'M NOT SURE ABOUT THAT SPOT EITHER.
FW
AP
HOW ABOUT...
DANG!
VOOSH

I KNEW KATSURŌ WOULD COME UP WITH SOMETHING.
SOUNDS GOOD.
...DIVIDING THE GOAL IN HALF...YOU DEFEND YOUR SIDE AND I'LL COVER MY SIDE?
DAICHI'S POSITION
KATSURŌ

FWAP
UP

NEXT.
NO ONE'S SCORED SO FAR.
BUT THE GROUP B GUY IS DOING JUST AS WELL. WHO'S HE?
THAT'S WHAT WE EXPECT FROM KATSURŌ!
YES.

AND TATSUYA, WHO WAS PERFECT ON THE TARGET TEST!
IT'S SEIJI FROM MUSASHI-NOMORI!
NOW, I WONDER WHAT KIND OF IMAGINATION THEY'LL SHOW US.
THE QUESTION IS HOW THEY'LL USE SEIJI.

VUP
SU
PGF

IT'S COMING!
DIVE
FUMP

DON'T WORRY!
DAICHI!
TUMP
BACK-WARDS !?
!
BIP

17
19
TATSUYA !!

THOOM
HERE'S THE SHOT!
17

FOO
SH
THEY USED SEIJI AS A DECOY, AND FOOLED US.
IT'S LOW. A GROUND SHOT!
GREAT!
THAT'S A DAVOR SUKER MOVE!
AWE-SOME!

WHISTLE!™

STAGE.105

Skill Test (Last Episode)

SEIJI, HUH? AND THE OTHER ONE IS TATSUYA, RIGHT?
IT WAS A MAKESHIFT TEAM, BUT THEY CAME UP WITH A KILLER PLAY.
THEY DID IT!

I PRACTICED IT A HUNDRED TIMES, BUT...
THAT'S AN OFFENSIVE PATTERN WE TRIED DURING THE HIBA MATCH.

FOR TATSUYA'S PRACTICAL SKILLS TO BECOME EFFECTIVE AT JOSUI...
...I NEED TO PLAY AT HIS LEVEL.

IT'S ENVIRONMENT THAT NURTURES EXCELLENT PLAYERS!
I UNDER-STAND WHAT COACH MEANT NOW.

...SEIJI PULLED IT OFF BETTER THAN I DID ON HIS FIRST TRY.
POSITIONING, PASSING AND SPEED...THE MAKE-UP OF A TEAM CAN MAKE SUCH A BIG DIFFERENCE.
NICE SHOT.
YOU TOO.

STAGE.105

Skill Test (Last Episode)

NICE TO MEET YOU.
THE BEST THING YOU CAN DO FOR ME IS STAY OUT OF THE WAY.
SAVE IT, B-TEAMER.
I ABSOLUTELY CANNOT LOSE THIS ONE.
HE'S THE DEFENDER, HUH?
EISHI!

SHŌ.
COME ON, SHŌ, BRING IT!
HOW WILL HE HACK IT AGAINST THE GUYS FROM THE YOUTH LEAGUE?

18
TUMP
YŪTO'S DRIBBLING !!
HE'S TAKING THE BALL IN ALONE!

YES!
MARK THE OTHER ONE!
LEAVE YŪTO!
YO OSH
I'LL TAKE CARE OF HIM!
...AND YOU'LL GET BURNED, YŪTO.
UNDER-ESTIMATE ME...
OUR ROLES ARE REVERSED NOW, HUH EISHI!?
HMPH.

IGNORING SHŌ, HUH?
HE THINKS THIS IS ALL ABOUT THE ELITES, I GUESS. WHAT ARROGANCE.
WHY ISN'T HE PASSING THE BALL TO SHŌ? HE'S OPEN!

NOT BAD, EISHI!!
SNEER
HOW ABOUT THIS!?
YOU WON'T SHAKE ME!
DA
YŪTO IS CUTTING BETWEEN TWO OF THEM!
SH

31
18
DASH
WHERE'S HE LOOKING?
GLANCE

VOOSH
TUMP
SHIFT
OPEN!
19
31

OH NO...
THAT IS ALL ME, BABY!
WHOA.
5
30

SMAP
KATSURŌ COVERED THE GOAL!
WAY TO GO!
NO GOOD.
HAVING TWO KEEPERS JUST ISN'T FAIR.

THAT KID!
FO
OM
SMAP

THAT GUY...
IT WAS THE GROUP B GUY THIS TIME!
THAT WAS CLOSE!
TUMP
NOW THAT YOU MENTION IT...
THIS TEAM'S HOLDING ITS OWN, HUH?
HUH?
HEY ...

...I WANT SOMEONE...
...TO BE...
WHEREVER...
!
FUMP
...HE'S ALWAYS THERE!

BAMP
WITHOUT REALIZING IT...

FKW
...I'VE STARTED FOLLOWING HIS LEAD!?
AM-P

PHFF
WHAT DO YOU THINK?
I GET IT NOW.
RAAH
SHŌ ...
...KAZA-MATSURI.
WHAT'S YOUR NAME?

WHISTLE!

STAGE.106 Lunch Time

THANKS.
OOPS?
FWIP
...
CHANGED MY MIND.
THAT WAS HOT!
NOT TOO SHABBY, I'D SAY.
HA
IT'S JUST LIKE HIM.

YOU ATTACKED THE BALL LIKE A PIT BULL TILL THE VERY END! VERY NICE!
NICE ASSIST!
I AGREE.
WHY GET ALL WORKED UP OVER A SKILL TEST.
GRAB
YOU'RE WRONG.
IT'S IMPORTANT TO HATE LOSING.
DOESN'T MATTER IF IT'S A GAME OR A DRILL.
THE FIRST-RATE PLAYERS ARE THE ONES WHO HATE LOSING THE MOST.

GRIN
THE SKILL TEST IS OVER!
AFTER LUNCH...
...WE'LL START AFTERNOON PRACTICE.
CAFETERIA
CHATTER
CHATTER

CAN I SIT HERE?
IS THAT SPOT OPEN?
JUST... OKAY.
HOW'D YOUR SKILL TESTS GO?
COUPE DU MONDE FRANCE 1998
SURE.

AH...ONE LEFT.
LESSEE HERE...

!
PUDDING

IS THIS FOOD FANCY ENOUGH FOR A RICH MOMMA'S BOY?
HEH

YOU WOULD KNOW.
SNORT

SNAG
PUDDING
PFFT.
♪
CLUMP
CLUMP
CLUMP

WHAT A WELL-BALANCED MENU.
SUGAR, FAT, VITAMINS, MINERALS AND PROTEINS.

JUNIOR HIGH STUDENTS ARE IN AN IMPORTANT GROWTH STAGE.
IT'S IMPORTANT TO EAT EVERYTHING ON YOUR PLATE.

YOU JUST MADE MY DAY!
WOW, SOMEONE UNDER-STANDS.

JUST RUN A LITTLE HARDER, KID.
THAT WILL ADD 130 UNNECCESSARY CALORIES.

I LIKE YOU. WHY DON'T YOU TAKE ONE ONE OF THESE, TOO.
PUDDING

HM?
CHECK IT.
KREEK
CLAKK
CHECK OUT THE GROUP AT THAT TABLE OVER THERE.
...WE'RE GETTING A LOT OF ATTENTION ...
IT FEELS LIKE...

BUT, I GUESS IT'S NATURAL.
PLOP
JOLT
HUH?
AFTER ALL, THESE GUYS ARE INCREDIBLE PLAYERS.
PLOP
TING

EAT YOUR OWN CARROTS.
SEIJI!
I LIKE CARROTS ANYWAY.
IT'S COOL.
KATSURŌ.
CUT IT OUT, OR I'LL MAKE YOU EAT THEM.
IF I CAN'T EAT IT, I CAN'T EAT IT.
SHUN
THAT LITTLE GUY SEEMS TO BE SEIJI'S FRIEND.
CELL MATES IN KATSURŌ'S JAIL.
YOU'RE SUCH A NICE GUY, SHŌ.
SHEESH.
SHUT UP!
MAYBE HE'S SOME BIG DEAL AFTER ALL?

IT'S EMBARRASSING TO BE HERE WITH A BUNCH OF LOSERS WHO JUST WANT TO SCREW AROUND AND HAVE FUN.
WE'RE IN THE MIDDLE OF A POWER RETREAT TO ESTABLISH A NEW TEAM.

AS OPPOSED TO SIMPERING BABIES WHO SIT AROUND AND COMPLAIN ABOUT EVERYTHING.

AREN'T YOU COACH SAIONJI'S PET MIDGET?
WHAT'S YOUR STORY, HUH? YOU'RE ONLY HERE BECAUSE YOU'VE GOT A CONNECTION.

STOP IT, KAZUMA. YOU HAVE A SHORT FUSE.
WHAT DID YOU SAY!?
SCOOCH

I'M HERE BECAUSE OF MY OBVIOUS PRACTICAL SKILLS. ARE YOU SUCH AN IDIOT THAT YOU CAN'T FIGURE THAT OUT?
WHAT!?
DOES THAT PASS FOR A PUT-DOWN WHERE YOU COME FROM?
MASH
MASH
TASTE
!
GLUGUG
SOY SAUCE OVER FRAN CARAMEL?
MUSH
MUSH

SAME HERE.
THIS CONVERSATION BORES ME.
NO, THANKS!
PLEASE DON'T MAKE ME LOOK AT IT.
YOU LIKE IT, DON'T YOU?
WANNA TRY?
GYUCCH

GLUNK
GLUNK
GLUNK

IT WORKS FOR ME.
HOW CAN YOU DRINK MILK WITH YOUR MEAL?
I CAN'T HAVE ANYTHING BUT GREEN TEA WITH RICE MYSELF.

COUPE DU MONDE
FRANCE
1998

READ THIS WAY
1998年
WE DIDN'T GET EVEN ONE WIN AT THE WORLD CUP.
...IT SEEMED OBVIOUS TO ME THAT JAPAN ISN'T READY FOR THE WORLD YET.
THEY SAY IT'S BECAUSE WE LACKED DECISIVE POWER... THAT THE TEAM WAS MIS-DIRECTED, ETCETERA, BUT...
1998年
BUT THEY'RE NOT UN-BEATABLE.
JAPAN CAN BECOME A LOT STRONGER.
THE OPPONENTS HAD PHYSICAL STRENGTH, SPEED, ACCURACY ...
PLUS THEY WERE MENTALLY TOUGH... THEY HAD NATIONAL PRIDE.

WELL, I'M NOT SO SURE. CROATIA BEAT US BY A GOAL WITH A VERY WEAK TEAM.

BESIDES, WE DEFENDED WELL AGAINST ARGENTINA.

WHAT ABOUT MEXICO, THEN?
PHYSICAL POWER IS THE DECIDING FACTOR, I SAY.
THEY MAKE A LOT OF UNNECESSARY MISTAKES, THOUGH.
SOME OF THE AFRICAN TEAMS HAVE AMAZING POWER, RIGHT?

SUGAR

FOR THEM, IT ISN'T A DREAM, BUT A REALITY.
AMONG US HERE, THERE ARE PLAYERS WITH ACTUAL INTERNATIONAL EXPERIENCE.

....TO THE OUTSIDE WORLD.
THIS TEAM OFFERS A DOOR...

...WANT TO BE A PART OF IT.
I ALSO ...

CHECK OUT THE LITTLE SOCCER NUTS OVER THERE.

WHOA.

WHAT'RE YOU SAYING? YOU'RE YOUNG TOO, AREN'T YOU?
THEY'RE TOTALLY OBSESSED WITH SOCCER. MAN, THEY'RE YOUNG.

THIS IS WEIRD.
WILL THEY TEACH US?
I WISH THEY'D LET ME KICK AROUND WITH THEM.

JOLT
HE'S A STAR PLAYER, MAEKAWA. HOSHIDA IS OVER THERE, TOO.

STAGE.107
The Lawn Is a Strong Enemy

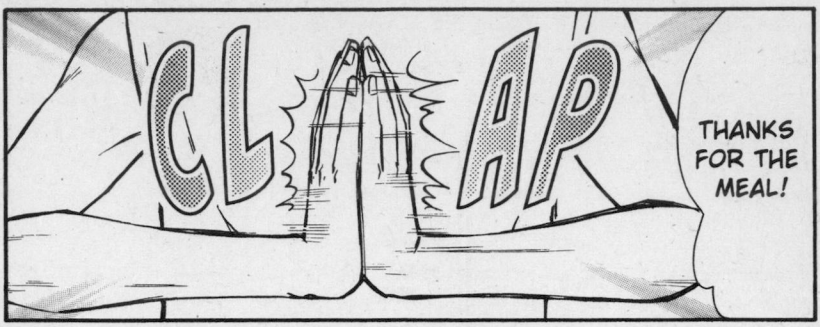
CLAP
THANKS FOR THE MEAL!

...I'M READY FOR IT!
NO MATTER WHAT THEY THROW AT US THIS AFTER-NOON...
BURRP
I'VE GOT SOME SERIOUS FUEL IN MY TANK.

...

ATHLETES NEED TO EAT LIKE PIGS!
WHAM

TAKI, ARE YOU STILL EATING? YOU'RE SO SLOW.
JUST LOOK AT THAT PUNY PORTION, TOO!

HUH?
THAT'S WEIRD.
YOU STILL HAVE SOME LEFT.
TEPPEI.
SPIN
NOW, LET'S PRACTICE.
POKE POKE

...
ARE YOU MESSING WITH HIM?
C'MON, LET'S GO.
WHAT IF MOM FINDS OUT?
NOT GOOD. I'D BETTER EAT EVERY-THING.
CHOMP CHOMP

PRACTICE AT LAST.
I WONDER WHAT WE'LL BE DOING.

UNLIKE OTHER COUNTRIES, JAPANESE PLAYERS...
...ONLY PLAY ON NATURAL TURF ONCE THEY TURN PRO.
BUT I GUESS IT SHOULDN'T BE A SURPRISE.
TSU-BASA.
WHY ARE YOU STANDING THERE LIKE A MORON!?
YOU SHOULDN'T GET SO EXCITED OVER SOMETHING LIKE A LAWN.

NATURAL TURF.
BEFORE WE DO ANYTHING, WE'VE GOT TO GET PAST THAT DIFFERENCE.
LET'S START THE PRACTICE. DIVIDE INTO A AND B GROUPS.
...WHILE MANY OF THE GROUP A GUYS PLAYED CLUB SOCCER ON TURF.
THE GROUP B PLAYERS HAVE ONLY PLAYED ON DIRT FIELDS ....
20

IS THIS DISCRIMINATION AGAIN?
WHAT THE HECK!?

GUYS IN GROUP A ARE PRACTICING MINI-GAMES AND FORMATIONS!

THAT'S NOT TRUE.
THEY'RE TRYING TO HUMILIATE US.

HOW COME GROUP B HAS TO PRACTICE PASSING?

JUST DO YOUR BEST.
THE BASICS ARE IMPORTANT.

?
VROOM
DON'T TOUCH ME, FOREIGN DEVIL!

MAKE A SOLID STOP BEFORE YOU KICK. IT IS VERY IMPORTANT. IT'S VERY EASY IN CONCEPT, BUT DIFFICULT IN PRACTICE.
THUP
THAT'S ALSO TRUE OF THE PASS. SHOOTING IS SIMPLY PASSING INTO THE GOAL.
FOOSH

TO PUT IT SIMPLY, SOCCER IS ALL ABOUT STOPPING AND KICKING.
TSUBASA.
BOOMP

A PASS IS A PIECE OF CAKE!
PIECE OF WHAT?
HE'S SAYING IT'S EASY.
HE HAS NO CLUE.
COME ON THEN! ♪
SHOW ME A SLICE OF CAKE, TEPPEI!
SNAP
ARE YOU MAKING FUN OF ME!!
NOW, YOU DIE!
THERE!
BOOM

TH-OOM
VIP
...
TO MY FEET.
YOU MUST PASS ACCURATELY...
HE'S QUICK!
NOT ONLY THAT...
SWAP
NO GOOD.
OKAY?
...IT'S A HARD PASS.

BURN
ALL RIGHT, ALL RIGHT! I GET IT.
ROLL
BIP
BIP
EVERY-ONE, TRY IT OUT!
BURN
BURN
THE BALL DOESN'T BOUNCE AS WELL AS IT DOES ON DIRT.
DON'T GIVE UP!
DANG IT!
C'MON!
HUH?
SHUT UP! LET ME TRY AGAIN.
WHAT'S THE MATTER?
BIP
BIP
20
BOOM

TO MAKE IT REACH, I NEED TO PUT MORE BEHIND IT.
JUST AS I THOUGHT.
THAT MEANS ...
...THAT PASSES I GET FROM OTHER PEOPLE ARE GOING TO COME AT ME HARDER.
!
SMACK
ROLL
IT'S DIFFICULT TO TRAP A HARD PASS.
SOCCER ON DIRT IS WAY DIFFERENT. THIS PRACTICE IS MORE IMPORTANT THAN I THOUGHT.
LOOKS LIKE THEY'RE STRUGGLING AGAINST THE TURF.

DON'T JUST THROW YOUR WATER EVERYWHERE!
AFTER YOU RINSE YOUR MOUTH, SPIT THE WATER OUT OF BOUNDS!
DON'T SPIT ON THE LAWN!
HEY, PUNKS!
IT'LL TAKE A WHILE BEFORE THEY GET USED TO IT.
SURE, WHAT-EVER.
WHAT DID YOU SAY?
MAN, WHAT A NAG!
MY LAWN IS NOT A GARBAGE BIN.
SOMEONE SPIT OUT GUM!
ARGH! DARN IT.
GEEZ.

I'M GETTING THE DISTANCE, BUT MY ACCURACY IS REALLY INCONSISTENT.
IT'S A GOOD PASS.
OOPS.
THERE YOU GO.
SWIP
!
TAKI, HOW DO YOU PASS SO ACCURATELY?
IT'S JUST TRIAL AND ERROR...
IF I HIT IT WITH THE RIGHT PART OF MY FOOT, THE BALL WILL GO WHERE I LIKE.
LIKE MY TOES: BIG TOE, SECOND TOE, MIDDLE TOE...
IN MY CASE, I THINK ABOUT WHAT PART OF MY FOOT TO USE AS I KICK.
LET ME SEE...
...I REPEAT IT OVER AND OVER SO I GET CONSISTENT RESULTS.
...AND ONCE I FIGURE OUT A TECHNIQUE ...

GROUP B IS PRACTICING PASSES?

SOME OF THEM ARE SULKING.
THE PRACTICE SESSION IS ALMOST OVER, BUT THEY'RE STILL ON BASIC SKILLS. EVEN I FEEL SORRY FOR THEM.

WELL, WELL. LOOK AT THEM!

BUT I HAVE A FEELING IT ISN'T JUST REMEDIAL TRAINING ...

HE'S KICKING MUCH BETTER THAN HE DID EARLIER.
YOU CAN PASS PROPERLY TWO OUT OF TEN TIMES NOW.
IS THAT RIGHT?
FOOM
YEAH.
SHOOP
ALREADY?
HA HA HA
WHAT?
PRACTICE OVER! LEAVE THE GROUNDS.
TWEE TWEE

TO KEEP IT IN GOOD CONDITION, WE LIMIT PRACTICE TO TWO HOURS IN THE MORNING AND TWO IN THE AFTERNOON... FOUR HOURS TOTAL.
THE LAWN IS ALSO ALIVE. IT TAKES A LOT OF ABUSE FROM ALL YOUR RUNNING AROUND.
OH, IT'S YOU...FROM THIS MORNING.
NOT QUITE SATISFIED YET, KID?
WHAT AN INTERESTING THING TO SAY, KID.
YOU'RE RIGHT. I'M SURE THE GRASS DOESN'T LIKE GETTING POUNDED BY CLEATS.
OKAY!
HIT THE SPRINKLERS.
IF YOU DON'T HAVE A RELATIONSHIP WITH THE GRASS, YOU CAN'T TAKE CARE OF IT.
YOU HAVE TO HAVE A SENSE FOR THE LAWN'S CONDITION... HOW IT FEELS ON THE SKIN.
THE GRASS IS TURNING DARK GREEN. PERHAPS IT NEEDS MORE WATER.
IF YOU INDULGE IT TOO MUCH, IT WILL TURN OUT TO BE NO GOOD. JUST LIKE WITH PEOPLE.

CHIR CHIR
I'VE BEEN WORKING WITH GRASS ALMOST 30 YEARS, BUT I'VE NEVER SAID "IT'S FINE THE WAY IT IS," YET.
IT'S JUST AN ENDLESS SEQUENCE OF TRIAL AND ERROR.

COMPARED TO FOREIGN COUNTRIES, JAPANESE SOCCER MAY STILL BE INFERIOR.
BUT I DON'T THINK OUR JAPANESE LAWN IS INFERIOR TO ANYTHING!
I'M PROUD OF THIS LAWN!

UNCLE, YOU...
HE'S PROUD OF THE WORK HE DOES.

...REMIND ME OF SOMEONE I KNOW. HE'S MY FRIEND AT AN ODEN STAND.
WA HA HA
I BET HE'S ALSO A STUBBORN OLD MAN.

12 IN THE DISTANCE (The End)

WHISTLE! THEATRE !!

Elegant People

MANGA BY SEKI, ASSISTANT S

Will you wait for him?

--Previously on "The Young and the Clueless"--

By MESO AIKO

Next in Whistle!

IN THE DISTANCE

Shô, Tatsuya and Daichi have been invited to try out for an all-star team that will compete on an international level. New and old rivals alike gather to vie for spots on the select team, but for Shô, it's gut-check time when he realizes that his technical skills are on the bottom end of the curve. Will he be able to make the cut?

Available September 2006!

SHONEN JUMP'S
NARUTO™

CHARACTER ILLUSTRATIONS

LEARN ALL THE SECRETS OF NARUTO'S UNIVERSE

- Available July 2006!
- $14.99
- 7-1/8" x 10-1/8"
- All in color!

EXCLUSIVE PINUP & MAP

CREATOR Q&A

Mysteries of the Village Hidden in the Leaves revealed!

Find out all the essentials to understanding episodes 1-37 of the *Naruto* anime series. Plus get exclusive insider information about the production of the show, including: character designs, interviews with creator Masashi Kishimoto and the voice actors, and an original pinup!

Separated into different story arcs, the profile book introduces all the main characters and their enemies. Packed with special color illustrations, this guide is indispensable for any Naruto fan—Believe it!

www.naruto.com

NARUTO -HIDEN-DOGAEMAKI- OFFICIAL ANIMATION BOOK
© 2003 by Masashi Kishimoto/SHUEISHA Inc.

THE REAL ACTION STARTS IN...

www.shonenjump.com

遊☆戯☆王
Millennium World
BIRTH OF THE BLUE-EYES WHITE DRAGON!
ONLY $7.95! EACH
VOL. 4 ON SALE AUG. 1!
ON SALE AT:
www.shonenjump.com
ALSO AVAILABLE AT YOUR LOCAL BOOKSTORE AND COMIC STORE.
RATED T FOR TEEN
SJ
viz media

遊☆戯☆王
DUELIST
VOL. 16 ON SALE AUG. 1!
YUGI VS. JONOUCHI:
DEATHMATCH BETWEEN
BEST FRIENDS!
SHONEN JUMP
MANGA
YU-GI-OH! © 1996 by Kazuki Takahashi/SHUEISHA Inc.

THE EPIC SHOWDOWN BETWEEN MAN AND FISH-MAN BEGINS!

Vol. 11
on sale now!

ONE PIECE
ONE PIECE™

ONE PIECE © 1997 by Eiichiro Oda/SHUEISHA Inc.

viz media

SHONEN JUMP™ MANGA

ON SALE AT:
www.shonenjump.com
ALSO AVAILABLE AT YOUR LOCAL BOOKSTORE AND COMIC STORE.

NARUTO © 1999 by Masashi Kishimoto/SHUEISHA Inc.

Tell us what you think about SHONEN JUMP manga!

Our survey is now available online.
Go to: ***www.SHONENJUMP.com/mangasurvey***

Help us make our product offering better!

BLEACH © 2001 by Tite Kubo/SHUEISHA Inc. NARUTO © 1999 by Masashi Kishimoto/SHUEISHA Inc.
DEATH NOTE © 2003 by Tsugumi Ohba, Takeshi Obata/SHUEISHA Inc. ONE PIECE © 1997 by Eiichiro Oda/SHUEISHA Inc.

SUBSCRIBE TODAY & BECOME A MEMBER OF THE SHONEN JUMP SUBSCRIBER-CLUB...

You'll get:

*Access to Exclusive Online Content!

*50% Savings Off the Newsstand Price!

*Exclusive Premiums!

All this available ONLY to Subscribers!

SHONEN JUMP

THE WORLD'S MOST POPULAR MANGA™

FILL OUT THE SUBSCRIPTION CARD ON THE OTHER SIDE, OR SUBSCRIBE ONLINE AT:

www.shonenjump.com

Save 50% off the newsstand price!

SHONEN JUMP™

THE WORLD'S MOST POPULAR MANGA

SUBSCRIBE TODAY and SAVE 50% OFF the cover price PLUS enjoy all the benefits of the SHONEN JUMP SUBSCRIBER CLUB, exclusive online content & special gifts ONLY AVAILABLE to SUBSCRIBERS!

☑ **YES!** Please enter my 1 year subscription (12 issues) to *SHONEN JUMP* at the INCREDIBLY LOW SUBSCRIPTION RATE of $29.95 and sign me up for the SHONEN JUMP Subscriber Club!

Only $29.95!

NAME

ADDRESS

CITY STATE ZIP

E-MAIL ADDRESS

☐ MY CHECK IS ENCLOSED ☐ BILL ME LATER

CREDIT CARD: ☐ VISA ☐ MASTERCARD

ACCOUNT # EXP. DATE

SIGNATURE

CLIP AND MAIL TO

SHONEN JUMP
Subscriptions Service Dept.
P.O. Box 515
Mount Morris, IL 61054-0515

Make checks payable to: **SHONEN JUMP.**
Canada add US $12. No foreign orders. Allow 6-8 weeks for delivery.

P6SJGN YU-GI-OH! © 1996 by Kazuki Takahashi / SHUEISHA Inc.